# SPIRITUAL HEALING

# SPIRITUAL HEALING

George E. Parkinson, D.D.

Introduction by
Norman Vincent Peale, D.D.

HAWTHORN BOOKS, INC.
*W. Clement Stone, Publisher*
*New York*

## ACKNOWLEDGMENT

The author is deeply indebted to these people for their kind assistance. Nancy J. Morrow read the entire manuscript and made helpful changes that improved both form and content of the book. Dorothy F. Kennedy read parts and offered valuable suggestions. I also thank the many others for their encouragement and interest in this work.

In preparation of the volume, the author received invaluable aid from William A. Pakan and his staff. And I express my sincerest gratitude to Dr. Norman Vincent Peale, who wrote the Introduction

SPIRITUAL HEALING

Copyright © 1971 by Hawthorn Books, Inc. Copyright under International and Pan-American Copyright Conventions. All rights reserved, including the right to reproduce this book or portions thereof in any form, except for the inclusion of brief quotations in a review. All inquiries should be addressed to Hawthorn Books, Inc., 260 Madison Avenue, New York, New York 10016. This book was manufactured in the United States of America and published simultaneously in Canada by Prentice-Hall of Canada, Limited, 1870 Birchmount Road, Scarborough, Ontario.

Library of Congress Catalog Card Number: 74-7855

ISBN: 0-8015-7036-0

1 2 3 4 5 6 7 8 9 10

# Table of Contents

## 1. My First Encounter With Spiritual Healing
Questioning Spiritual Healing Personally
My First Spiritual Healing Service

## 2. Four Vital Premises About Spiritual Healing
What is Spiritual Healing?
1. Purpose
2. Wholeness
3. Body, Mind, and Spirit
4. The Spiritual Force

Personal Conclusions

## 3. Biblical Background of Healing
Divine Intervention
1. The Ten Commandments
2. Prophets
3. Jesus Christ

## 4. The One Word Which Heals
   Three Types of Love
      1. Eros
      2. Philos
      3. Agape
   Loving Hands
   Healing Through Love
      1. Home
      2. Neighborhood
      3. Church
      4. Community
      5. Conclusions

## 5. The Three D's of Healing
      1. Desire
      2. Dynamic
      3. Deliverance

## 6. Questions and Answers

To Hazel, Bob, Jim,
Kim, and Eric

# INTRODUCTION

Depth of understanding and balance of judgment are required to author a competent book on spiritual healing. If one believes in the phenomenon at all—and well he should—he must approach the subject with scientific objectivity as well as faith.

One can, of course, dilute such a book so that it comes off merely as a psychosomatic treatment; one that shows the beneficial effect of healthy mental states on well-being.

But a comprehensive work on spiritual healing in all of its ramifications must believe and demonstrate that God does for a fact heal, even though the process by which the healing is accomplished is not clear and may seemingly even defy accepted scientific procedures.

George Parkinson has achieved admirable balance in his treatment of spiritual healing. That he is a believer is, of course, obvious, but his manner of approach is one of common sense and complete objectivity all the way. The combination of faith and science so perfectly demonstrated in the author lends complete credibility to the book.

The book is solidly based on scripture, which, for the spiritually-minded reader, greatly enhances the authenticity of the work. The time has long since gone by when any author should apologize or be diffident about writing on the subject of spiritual healing. Men such as George Parkinson have lifted the phenomenon into the category of respectability in the entire healing process of mankind. Medicine generally recognized its validity today, and the relationship between doctors and pastors has deepened across the years. This book will add to the validity of the subject, and I foresee that "Spiritual Healing" by

Dr. George E. Parkinson will have a worthy place in the growing literature on the subject.

Dr. Parkinson, an old and honored friend, has filled his book with fascinating illustrations out of his wide experience. He writes with rare charm. His book is very readable and interesting and, may we also say, convincing.

Norman Vincent Peale

"He that believeth on me, the works that I do shall he do also; and greater works than these shall he do;"

(John 14:12)

"When ye call I will hear and will answer speedily."

(Psalms 102:2)

"Whatsoever ye shall ask in prayer, believing, ye shall receive."

(Matthew 21:22)

"And the prayer of faith shall save the sick, and the Lord shall raise him up. ."

(James 5:15)

# 1

## My First Encounter With Spiritual Healing

I DON'T KNOW with what depth you know about spiritual healing, so I must treat the subject as though you are neophytes. In this way we can come to a common ground. At once let me establish the fact that spiritual healing is NOT MAGIC. It is not something of a "mumbo-jumbo" attitude toward life. It is not believing God to be a "sort of a pill bottle" for us, such as taking an aspirin when we have a headache. It is not prayer in a sense that we are using prayer as a vehicle by which we escape the reality of life. Spiritual healing, in my estimation, is getting away from that which is the "risque" in the field of religion and philosophy and theology and getting into the practical and the respectable and the dignified area which I am sure our Lord intended it to be in everything that he says about *wholeness* in the New Testament. I suspect the best way for me to launch the subject then is to give you my own introduction to spiritual healing.

Eight years ago if anyone had said to me, "Sir, I want you to become vitally interested in spiritual healing," I think it might have been exciting to hear the answer that I would have given. At that time I was about as uninterested in the subject as anyone could possibly be. Now, this was not because I had not read the New Testament. This was not because I did not believe in the miracles of Jesus, but it happened to be that I belonged to that area of what we call modern trained clergy and theologians. We were taught that the miracles of Jesus had come forth at a particular given time, and now in such a wonderful scientific age when there are such vast and magnificent things being done in the fields of psychology, psychiatry, and medicine, we no longer need the miracles of Jesus.

Well, I had swallowed this and had really fostered this in my own thinking and history, but suddenly a friend of mine, a medical doctor in my congregation, began to kind of elbow me. If someone other than a physician had done this, I probably could have passed it off without much difficulty, but he was a respectable eye surgeon, opthalmologist, and had a very excellent reputation in our community in the medical society. I even investigated him after he began to agitate me on the subject. I began to talk to some of his friends to see whether or not he might have "flipped his lid" somewhere along the line and might have gotten in some sort of trouble. No, I found out that he was among the most highly respected eye surgeons in the community. In fact, one of the surgeons, one of his own craft, whom I talked with, said to me, "I would probably, if I was going to have anything done in the area of the eye, turn to this man because I have so much confidence in him." Well, this intrigued and thrilled me!

I was getting ready to go to a meeting in Chicago. I don't know whether any of you have to or find it a necessity to travel the Pennsylvania Railroad, and I hope the employees of the railroad will not feel ill toward me, but in our area it is not smooth, not at all. And between Canton, Ohio and Chicago it is anything but smooth. Well, I got a bedroom to go on this particular evening, and the train goes through Canton about 1:30 A.M. and gets into Chicago about 8:30 the next morning. When I went to the station, the doctor gave me Emily Gardner Neale's book *A Reporter Finds God Through Spiritual Healing*. Now if any of you want a primer which will introduce you to spiritual healing, this is the book I highly recommend as the first book you ought to read on the subject. To be truthful with you I did not intend to read the book at all. I had it in my briefcase along with two other books, and I wanted desperately to read one of those other books. As I sat down and kicked my shoes off, I thought, "Well, I'll get out this other book and read a little bit because I'll never go to sleep now." So, I reached in my briefcase and didn't pay much attention to the book I had pulled out, and I pulled out *A Reporter Finds God Through Spiritual Healing*.

I thought since I had it in my hand, I couldn't do any worse than read the introduction, so I started. Somewhere in Indiana about 3:30 or 4 the next morning, I finished the book. It was a shock! This is where my introduction to Spiritual Healing began. It is also where my healing began to take place personally, for I can justify to you very generously today that I needed this and didn't know that I needed it.

A great many of you who have great need in your life, in your mind, in your body, and in your soul are not conscious of it at all, and I am your friend because I lived like this for so long without being conscious of any need in my life at all until I read this book and began to get interested in the subject.

I thought I was fairly intelligent. I knew I was physically very healthy, and I would deny and argue with anyone who thought I had any spiritual problems. And so would most of you! It is because, you see, if you can move around, you have the feeling that at least you're existing. But God never intended for us to *exist*. HE INTENDED FOR US TO "LIVE," VIBRANTLY. He intended for us to be *alive* all of the time we are living. This is the thing that many of us miss.

We are bogged down with one kind of a worry or frustration or inhibition or one thing and another. We think we have mental health. Most of us go through life half of the time mentally "sick," but we really do not recognize it, nor would we admit we are sick enough for psychiatric help or sick enough to even ask a psychologist whether or not there is something wrong with us. So we go through life limping mentally, when really there is much for us in the whole concept if we would only grab it and take hold of it and keep it. In the area of the spirit, most of us are religious. I suppose all of you are members of a church. You have, for a long time, professed a religion of one kind or another, but does it do anything for you? Is it exciting? Does it become real in your life? Does it make you interested in everything that goes on in the world?

# My First Encounter

## *Questioning Spiritual Healing Personally*

As I got to Chicago, I was sure that I now had been impressed enough that I had to do something about this whole matter of spiritual healing in my own life, as far as my own interest was concerned. First of all, I began then to look into life. There were two questions that as a Presbyterian I had to answer. Those of us who are Presbyterians have to be sure that the thing is Biblically rooted and theologically respectable of all things. This I had to get immediately settled in my mind.

Is this whole idea of spiritual healing Biblically valid? Is it respectable and dignified in the Bible, in the Old and the New Testament? I began a very thorough study of this. Yes, I found out very quickly that surprisingly much of the New Testament deals with healing. In the Gospels, for example, in the Acts of the Apostles, we have one happy chapter after another just "crammed" with the notion of spiritual healing. The period of the Old Testament in the very beginning, God sets out a purpose for us as individuals, and He continues all through man's history. Further on I have devoted an entire chapter to the Biblical background.

Was this theologically respectable? I took the three great principles of our theology as Christians: The Incarnation, the Atonement, and the Resurrection, and what it is our Lord is saying to us in these three. In each of these dramatic incidents in the life of our Lord, we find spiritual healing is rooted exactly for man's wholeness. That is why the following: "God came in Christ, the word made flesh," "God was in Christ, reconciling the world unto Himself," and "Because He lived, you and I too shall live."

## SPIRITUAL HEALING

The over-arching purpose of God is life. It is quality of life, not length of life. The entire idea of healing enters into the picture in the theological manner.

### *My First Spiritual Healing Service*

After having settled with that, I then called my doctor friend, and we agreed that he would take me to a healing service. Now this was looked upon with some anxiety by me because I suppose those of you who do not know the healing ministry as far as the Episcopal Church, Presbyterian, Lutheran, or United Church of Christ, would think of it as belonging to a kind of emotional group of people who bless handkerchiefs and get mixed up in all kinds of detours as far as the dignified church is concerned. This was exactly my concept of healing. You see, I didn't hear it in words . . . . *spiritual healing*. All I heard was *healing*. And if you're going to understand what spiritual healing is all about, you're going to have to lay great emphasis upon this word *spiritual*. Well, I called my doctor friend and told him I would be glad to go with him. On a Wednesday morning some weeks after this, a dreary Wednesday morning, we started out for a neighboring community where there was a healing service in an Episcopal Church. I have great respect for the Episcopalians, one reason being the great opening, the new vista, the new horizen they made possible for me and so many others to see. And when history is written of the spiritual healing movement some years hence from now, it will certainly give credit to the Episcopal Church for having really interested the Christian Church of the last half of the Twentieth Century in the spiritual healing ministry.

The doctor and I set out for the church on this

## My First Encounter

dreary, damp morning. As we were driving the 30 miles, I never let him know exactly what was going through my mind, but I can remember it very clearly. I thought, "Well, I know just what will happen! There will be a few little old ladies at the service, and that is all there will be. It won't be a very interesting service because the rector will get up, read out of a prayer book, give a few staid remarks about the Eucharist, conduct a Eucharistic service, and then invite everyone up for the laying on of hands. Everyone will go up . . . . except Doc and myself! And that will be all there is to it. After we leave, we'll evaluate what had taken place."

Finally we arrived. Sure enough, **there were those 15 little old ladies!** But let me make clear that those ladies would have been there if it were a rummage sale, bake sale, Bible class, or anything else going on. Whether it made any difference to the world, those little old ladies would be there, the vanguard of the Lord, meeting when the doors were open.

Well, there it was. With all my notions and doubts beforehand, there were those little old ladies. But I was to be greatly surprised, for just before the service started, a pleasant looking, young couple came in. I was a little taken back as I thought, "Now, what are they doing here? They don't have any business here. I wonder what they came about." (I found out later that at one of the services, this young lady had been healed of a very serious predicament in her life, and they had come back to give praise to God for the healing that had taken place in her life.) As the service went on, I was only partly right. There had been the little old ladies, but the rector did not read out of a prayer book, and it was a rather stimulating service.

## Spiritual Healing

I was much excited when the invitation came for the Eucharist as the rector said, "In the area of spiritual healing, we do not know anything about closed communion, so any of you who profess Christ as Lord and Master are invited in His name to come and partake of these elements." This was an interesting invitation because it was only the second time I had ever been invited to a Communion Rail in the Episcopal Church. I felt I had received some benefits from that Eucharistic exercise, and after we returned to our seats, the rector read a few passages.

Then there came the part I had been waiting for as we were invited to come up for the laying on of hands. I can remember distinctly looking over at the doctor to see what he was going to do. He was looking straight ahead, and as he usually does, not showing any emotion as to what he might have on his mind.

Thinking the only way to get him out of his revelry was to elbow him, I nudged him and asked jokingly, "Well, shall we go?"

"Well of course we're going!" he replied as he got up.

Standing in the aisle waiting for me to get out of the pew, he left me nothing to do but to get up and follow. After all, I didn't want to embarrass those 15 little old ladies, and mainly I didn't want to embarrass myself. Following directly behind the ladies, we went up and knelt right in the center of the altar.

The healing service began! My mind was entirely open to everything that was going on as I knelt listening to the prayer. It seemed like a very formal prayer, as later I discovered why. Everyone was kneeling with their heads bowed and eyes closed as the rector proceeded from one person to another. Suddenly I felt

## My First Encounter

his hands upon my head, and I could feel a very visible shaking of his hands .... so I peeked. (I'm human, you know.) I peeked to see just what was going on. I wanted to see. Then I thought, "He probably recognizes I am a clergyman, and he's 'giving me the business.' He's really going to put this thing on for all its worth." I looked very carefully, and there was nothing. His eyes were shut, and he was very calm. I bowed my head again, and just as soon as I had it bowed, again was the shaking. This really bothered me. He passed on to the next person, and soon the service was over.

Afterward the doctor and I spoke with the rector, and he said, "I didn't recognize you at all. A very interesting thing happened when I put my hands on your head. For the first time in my experience in the practice of spiritual healing, *I couldn't get my hands off!* This interested me because I saw you peek, and I didn't blame you. I was beginning to get a little concerned myself. But in a moment I was released."

The one thing which came to me at that moment was a strange *giving over* of myself. I knew in a very real way that my doubt was over. I knew the church, the established church, had to take an honest look at the whole matter of spiritual healing.

This led me to form an opinion about three maxims of our Lord's teaching, and these you will always need to know if you are going to understand the meaning of spiritual healing. Our Lord said to His disciples, "Go preach. Go teach. Go heal."

Now for 1500 years the church did all three of these in some way or another, but only in the first 300 years did the early church do effectively the healing ministry. For all the rest of the time, 1500 years, the ministry of healing languished in the Church of Jesus Christ. In the middle of the 19th century, Spiritual Healing again, in a small way, became a part of the church.

One hundred years ago the teaching of Mary Baker Eddy came out with Christian Science. For some years I was chairman of a committee from the United Presbyterian Church in the U.S.A. with the Christian Science Church on the general subject of the healing ministry of the church. At one of the luncheons of this combined committee, one of their leaders said, "It is quite unlikely Christian Science would ever have come into being had the established church a hundred years ago shown an interest in healing." Mary Baker Eddy could not find in her church that for which she was seeking. This is interesting only from the angle which helps us to point out today that there are more than 700 churches of all denominations conducting regular healing services in every one of the 50 states.

"Go thy way; thy faith hath made thee whole."

(Mark 10:52)

# 2

## Four Vital Premises About Spiritual Healing

### What is Spiritual Healing?

IT IS OBEDIENCE to God's will for man's wholeness which follows from faith in God's promises. How many of you really believe that God intended us to be whole? When asked a question of this nature, we discover it cannot be answered if we do not understand *wholeness*.

We need to understand that God created man in His own image. Can you imagine God being less than whole? Can you imagine God less than honest? It means then, you see, completeness. Man is made by God to be complete.

How does this completeness come about? It may be described by a Greek word, "salvus," which is literally translated "salvation." In every instance in the New Testament where the word *wholeness* occurs, you will find it translated with the word "salvus." You may use the words salvation and wholeness interchangeably.

Wholeness then means a right and perfect relationship with God in Christ. Now what we are talking about is as basic and as rudimentary as anything we have in our Christian theology. Then why did we ever let this get out of the church if it is so superior and seems to be a "side-show" of the very factual and rudimentary in the life of the Gospel? I do not have the answer to that, frankly. I simply raise the question. I am dedicated to the purpose as long as I have life to see that what our Lord said to us, "Go preach, go teach, go heal," happens in the life of the church, because it is within that institution that I believe we find the secret for all of life.

There are four things that seem to me to be of vital importance as we think about Spiritual Healing.

### 1- PURPOSE OF SPIRITUAL HEALING

The basic purpose of Spiritual Healing is to deepen one's relationship with the living Christ. I cannot emphasize that too much.

Spiritual and moral relativity and wholeness is, of course, an answer of every living Christian. Your relationship to Christ is of the utmost importance to you and to all others about you, for if that relationship is unsure and your devotion to Christ is a matter of question, then somewhere along the line you are going to develop a "soul sickness." It may be revealed in various ways. It may come out in your attitude toward others. It certainly will come out in your spiritual aridness.

What we are emphasizing here as basic to everything else is the understanding that man's relation to

## Four Vital Premises

God through Christ is essential to his wholeness as a mortal being.

### 2- WHOLENESS

The second thing we want to know is that God wills wholeness for all his creation. God wills wholeness for everyone. Do you believe it? What do we mean when we say "all creation?" I do not mean only *man*. Some of you may have read, not very long ago, that scientific article where a very eminent entomologist° went to work on doing certain things with plant life and biological life. He took a group of pansies and placed them in a box. He thereon took the same number and planted these in another box. On the first one they experimented with prayer. The other they did not pray about at all. Within a period of 2 months, the pansies that were prayed about that they may have growth and may have God's will in them were *six weeks ahead of those that had no prayer at all*. Think about this seriously.

Under the guise of some silly Presbyterian preacher talking to you, this is from the annuls recorded inside a scientific journal. If prayer is effective, then you see God wills wholeness for all His creation, and we must not think of ourselves as being so particular in God's creation as to feel that no other order of creation has God's interest. Now if God wills wholeness for all His creation, then we need to take one other step, and that is that He certainly wills that wholeness for you and for me.

This seems to me to be an exciting adventure. If you can understand that God wants you to be whole, it is

---
°Zoologist dealing with insects

something *more* than saying, "God wants me to be well." There is quite a difference between being well and being whole, and we need to define that very carefully as we go along.

## 3- BODY, MIND, AND SPIRIT

One of the basic postulates of spiritual healing is that man is basically ignorant of body, mind, and spirit closely linked together.

During the 19th Century the human being was regarded by science almost exclusively as a material object. Medicine during this time was, above all, materialistic. There were three very interesting men at work then: Freud, Adler, and Jung. Each of them brought into the "materia medica" the notion that there was something more than simply body to be treated. There was the treatment of a person whose mind works in such capacity when he is ill as to affect further his body illness. It is through these great psychiatrists that we got psychosomatic medicine.

Almost all physicians have read *Weiss and English*, which is the basic textbook in psychosomatic medicine. This also has become in the last 25 years the accepted book in our seminaries since it deals with understanding human personality, therefore most of our clergy have read this book. Just 25 years ago Weiss and English came out with this book titled *Psychosomatic Medicine*, which is now a textbook in almost every respectable seminary, thus encouraging the young theological neophytes to be sure to understand the human personality enough to recognize that it is psychosomatically oriented.

Well, we have a much faster way to get to it if our seminaries will only hear it and adhere to it. What we really are talking about in psychosomatic medicine is that *man is a person*. He is not a mind; he is not a body; he is not a soul; and this is exactly the way Jesus, if you will notice in every modern miracle, treated a human being. He treated them as a person. If you and I could get that concept, then we could understand more deeply what we are talking about in the area of Spiritual Healing.

### 4- *THE SPIRITUAL FORCE*

The last premise vital to our thinking of Spiritual Healing is that there is a positive, reconciling God providing a spiritual force which is available for you and for me in our time.

Coupled with this, let me mention one important thing. Along with every successful spiritual healing incident and service is the undergirding by very sincere, dedicated prayer. If you are going to be interested in the subject at all, you must first of all be interested in the subject of prayer, for prayer and spiritual healing are so closely allied that it seems almost impossible in my area of thinking to divorce one from the other.

**We have had magnificent experiences for twelve** years in our church in this area of intercessory prayer. If you are going to understand spiritual healing, you will seek to understand the meaning of intercession.

Oh, how conveniently we talk around the term intercessory prayer, but I wonder if we really do know what it means. Intercessory prayer means prayer in behalf of another or others, but it means something more than just having sympathy for your neighbor who is ill, and something more than prayer about the problems of people in your neighborhood. It means that you are willing to take his burden and lift it completely from his shoulders and put it on your own. It means that you are willing to get down on your knees and pray, not for 5 minutes, but all day if necessary, or all night if need be. You see, whatever you are actually asking God to do, you do not let go until you are as sure as Jacob wrestling with the angels, "unless I know, I will not let you go." And old Jacob went throughout all his life with a holy limp because this was his reminder that God had answered faithfully his prayer.°

If you and I are willing to be intercessors, then magnificent things can happen. Let me share with you one experience. A mother had been coming to our healing service on Thursday evenings for some time. For a month her daughter had been out of work simply because she could not continue due to some strange malady that doctors had not diagnosed for sure. She had many tests in the hospital, but no answer was found for it. On this particular evening as the mother came to the kneeling rail and hands were laid upon her head, she happened to look at her watch . . . . it was 7 minutes after 8. Upon going to her home, her daughter met her at the door, and the mother said to her, "What are you doing out of bed? You are supposed to be in bed."

The daughter replied, "Well, at about 5 after 8 this evening a very strange thing happened to me. I felt very strong! I felt hungry for the first time in a month. I went out and toasted some bread, poached some eggs, and made some coffee. And Mother, I feel just wonderful!"

The mother, as most of us who have had experience

---
°Genesis 32:24-32

## Four Vital Premises

in spiritual healing, was amazed, and very true is this amazement and ought never be classed as doubt when you say, "Well, I'd never believe it!" For that is telling the truth. The mother thus said to the daughter, "I think you had better not press your luck too far," and tried immediately to thwart what had already taken place in her life, which is really the work of the devil in us that immediately when God does something for us, frequently that old devil (or whatever you want to call him . . . . I have my own pet name for him) comes along and tries to undo everything that is done.

The daughter, stronger than the mother in this case, said, "No, I'm going to work in the morning."

"You're going to work in the morning?"

"Yes, I'm going to work," she reiterated.

The mother finally consented if she would call the doctor, so the daughter called, and the doctor said, "No, you are not going to work in the morning; at least not until I come around to see you."

"Well, I'll be damned!" were the exact words the doctor replied as he examined her thoroughly. "I guess you can go to work. I can't answer it, but there is no reason in the world for me to keep you at home since everything checks out perfectly. But I want to tell you one thing. If you get any other symptoms like you had before, you get home as fast as you can and call me at my office."

Well, that was at least 6 years ago, and the daughter has not come home to call the doctor yet. She accepted what happened as a healing through intercessory prayer, even though she was not present. The mother believes, of course, that this is exactly what happened.

## Spiritual Healing

### *PERSONAL CONCLUSIONS*

I would like to share with you my belief in Spiritual Healing. I believe God does come at the very center of our greatest need. What I actually believe, and you may think it extravagant, is that we would not be in the problem that we are in in the world today if those of us who are really Christian had put into practice what we actually read in our Bibles for so many, many years. We have been Bible-oriented, but have not been Biblically literate. Because of this Biblical illiteracy, we have taken from the pulpit, taken from our Sunday School teachers, taken from our theologians, and like sponges we have saturated ourselves with the truth they have given us, but we never did anything about the "sponge material." We have never really squeezed the sponge and shared what we have learned, or if we have really learned it, it did not sink deeply enough into us that we have put it into practice.

I want anyone who hears me to know that God intends no longer for you to go through life fabricating the truth of His Gospel by limping around spiritually half dead, physically moaning and groaning, and mentally complaining and griping about what goes on in our world. God, come in Jesus Christ, can change the world. He has brought this Gospel to you and to me, the Gospel of love and life and wholeness. He intends that you and I shall be ambassadors of that life, therefore you must claim this wholeness for yourself. You must appropriate the promises which God has made in His word until you feel the vibrancy of your spirit coming into your life making you complete. It starts, you see, within. Sometimes it starts almost imperceptibly. I can give you many examples

## Four Vital Premises

of people who have come kneeling and asking God to do this particular thing for them, "Take away this arthritis from me, please, Lord." They get up the same way as when they knelt. But a strange thing takes place the next day. They begin to discover that their world looks differently from what it did before. There is a certain kind of buoyancy that they cannot describe, for God has gone to work, you see, on the inner nature.

God will not heal you of arthritis and leave stinginess of spirit, fractiousness of nature, spuriousness in our minds, and hate against others in our hearts. These are appalling predicaments, and we suffer all kinds of physical ailments simply because we will not allow His therapeutic touch to work on our human spirit. Therefore, as we begin our next day, let each of us now affirm that God wants us to be whole and that He has the ability to do what He says because of His promise, because of His Divinity, and because of his uniqueness.

"In all thy ways acknowledge him, and he shall direct thy paths."
(Proverbs 3:6)

# 3

## *The Biblical Background of Healing*

Now and again one runs into a person who proclaims, "Spiritual Healing is certainly all right, I am sure, but I can't substantiate it as far as Scripture is concerned." To those of us who are engaged in the healing ministry of the church, there is a great danger of our becoming sensitive and impatient with a person like this, and frequently in our haste to answer, we convey a spirit contrary to that which is convincing to the agnostic.°

I suppose there is no subject in all religion where we have more agnosticism than we do in the area of Spiritual Healing. There are not many atheists° in this

---

° agnostic—one who withholds belief because he does not know and is unwilling to accept as proof, the evidence of revelation and spiritual experience.
° atheist—one who denies the existense of God

## SPIRITUAL HEALING

field, but we have questions asked by a great many people who are repeatedly saying, "I just don't know." Those who are interested in healing must indeed be very sympathetic with these people. It is not easy for one's emotion to simply believe in God, who is not seen but becomes clearly evident in the mystery of the working of His hand upon lives of those who are committed to Him. Those who have had the experience of laying on of hands or having experienced its result can very frequently become impatient with those who do not quickly see what we are talking about or do not agree with us. We would, therefore, plead with anyone who is going to concern himself with Spiritual Healing to first take time to patiently research the Scriptures to see what really is said about the matter of healing. Our Lord said, "My word is the seed, it is the seed of the Divine Life."

The person who seeks healing must be sure from God's word that his healing is assured, or he may try to reap a harvest where there is no seed planted. We would, of course, smile with some humor at the farmer who would attempt to reap a harvest in the field where he had forgotten to plant the seed. GOD DOES NOTHING WITHOUT HIS WORD. In the Psalms you will find these three statements:

> "He sent His word and it healed them."
> "Ye shall know the truth,"
> "and the truth shall make you free." (John 8:32)

These promises that God has given us in His Word are also familiar to you from the Scriptures:

> "Seek ye first the Kingdom of God and His righteousness, and all things shall be added unto you."
> "Seek and ye shall find."

## BIBLICAL BACKGROUND

"Knock and it shall be opened unto you."
"If you ask anything in my name and believe you shall receive it, it shall be done unto you."

These are promises with which you and I have lived throughout our lives. From the time we have known anything, we have known these verses. I have selected only a very few of those which are the most familiar. *One out of every seven verses in the Gospel has something to do with Spiritual Healing. One out of every fourteen verses in the Act of the Apostles has something to do with Spiritual Healing.* This surely would indicate that we have overlooked the importance of healing in our reading of the Scriptures. If we are going to accept God's promises and if we are going to believe what He says, we must then conclude, if we are logical and intelligent people, that God intends us to be whole. In that wholeness He intends to work at every area of our lives.

We know freedom from illness as we know the truth about God. If we are still fragmenting God into our little individual compartments and making Him serve our whims and our fancies, then we will always be perplexed about the matter of wholeness. Until we can accept God as one whose love is so extreme that you will go to any end in order to achieve His purpose for our lives, we do not know the God and Father of our Lord Jesus Christ, for it is in Him we see God perfectly revealed. It is in Him and His workings that we see the love and grace and mercy of God so very effectively put forth into practical application of the time in which we live.

No sinner will ever become a Christian if he does not know God wills it for his life to be free from sin. No person can experience re-generation in his life who has any doubt whatsoever that God would rather he not continue to be in his lost state.

I remember many years ago when I was a student pastor, I did the audacious thing of holding a two week revival meeting while I was a student in college. We learn things as we grow and develop in experience. I did this because the Elders of this rural church where I was serving had the custom of having services and were perfectly willing to invite someone in to do this, but I, thinking it was a rather a heavy burden on them financially, thought *I* should do it. Suffice it to say, we got along. I remember one particular experience which I am relating to you in connection with those services.

On an invitation one evening to come forward, one of my friends joined me, and as we talked, he said, "But I want some particular demonstration. I have got to know without any doubt in my mind whatsoever that God has touched my life and made me whole, that God has saved me."

Well, I tried everything I knew, but to no avail. He simply had to have some demonstration that God had come down to do something for him.

"Don't you believe in God?" I asked.
"Yes," he replied, "I believe in God."
"Don't you believe in the fact that God, once you have said you believe in him, can take your life and change it?"
"Yes," he answered, "I believe all that, but I want to *know* Him."
I finally in desperation said to him, "What do you want, God to slap you in the face so that you'll know you're safe?"
His reply was "I think it's something like that."

Now, how many of you have been slapped by God in

## Biblical Background

the face so that you would know that you had an experience of redemption? Not many, if any, I imagine. But if you were, WOULD YOU KNOW AND ACCEPT THAT IT WAS FROM GOD? This is not at all to deny the cataclysmic conversion experience or that dynamic central experience that comes to many people, but to most of us, God comes more quietly than this. To many of us if He came in that way, we would be doubting or rationalizing all the rest of our lives as to whether or not it was some unexplainable physical experience or a real genuine experience of the love of Christ coming into our spirit and into our soul. When we talk about the healing ministry Biblically, we must rely strictly on the truth of what the Bible says about it and not get led off on tangents which again and again appear by our own interpretation.

What I am trying to express is that for someone to say, "I believe God is able to heal me," without knowing from God's word that He *is willing* to heal him is like saying "I know there is a way from here to Jamestown." But refusing to get on that road and go there, you could stay exactly where you are forever and talk about Jamestown and the way to get there, but never make the journey. If you never make the attempt, you would then never be able to say "I know" or be trustworthy in the experimental end of the journey. Many of us have this difficulty, don't we, in our religious life?

We want great experiences from God, and God has promised to give us a "bushel load" of these experiences, but we still talk about wanting them but never do anything to really adventure as to whether or not God will come through for us.

## Spiritual Healing

It is the Gospel which the Holy Spirit says is the power of God unto salvation, both physical and spiritual. The Bible begins with God acting as a Creator. When He created man, He apparently had great magnificent plans for this creature.

> "And God said, Let us make man in our image, after our likeness: and let them have dominion over the fish of the sea, and over the fowl of the air, and over the cattle, and over all the earth, and over every creeping thing that creepeth upon the earth.
> So God created man in his *own* image, in the image of God created he him; male and female created he them."°

The word of God is quite clear in this message.... that man was the peer of all created beings. "Little lower than the Angels." He was originally intended to live a perfect state cosmos.

Whatever one may make out of the garden of Eden° in the textual material of the Bible, one certainly sees there the symbolism of a perfect estate, a cosmos, i.e. a world in which man has perfect harmony. Now Sin intervened, and man's choice of the lesser brought him into a state of unwholeness or chaos. (Genesis 3) These two words, cosmos and chaos, are always very interesting to treat in the healing ministry. If you go back for just a brief moment to the Eden story, you will see here Satan's declaration of war against God. As Satan comes in the form of a serpent tempting Eve, he says, "What is going on here that I see?"

"We have been told," she replied, "that we cannot

---

° Genesis 1:26-27
° Genesis 2:8

## BIBLICAL BACKGROUND

eat of the tree that is in the center of the Garden, the tree of good and evil, or we will die." (Death in the spiritual sense is the absence of wholeness or cutting off of the chance of living in the creation which God has given us to want).

"Oh, this is surely not the truth. I tell you that once you eat of the fruit of that tree in the midst of the Garden, you shall be as gods," the devil said.

And this was a temptation too great for a creature. If I should say to you now, "I could create about you the ability of divinity, of supremacy over everything in your life," you would be tempted, wouldn't you? The temptation is the experience which creates unwholeness in our lives, and Eve took from the tree in the center of the Garden and at once knew she had done something wrong.

When the man comes along and yields to the temptations of Eve, God comes and says to the first parents, "What has happened here?" You ladies ought to be really angry at this story. Good old Adam says, "The woman you gave to be with me, she is the one who has caused all of the trouble."

And here we have in the Bible the first record of what we call the "buck passer." We never want to accept the responsibility for what we do ourselves. This is so true as we see it in the healing ministry of the church.

Often and again people will say to me when I sit to talk with them about some problem, "My doctor has failed. I have paid him all kinds of money. He is supposed to be a skilled physician, but he has not been able to do anything for me." I can immediately recognize that that conviction is in the person's mind. When you say he has done nothing, that is a stretch of the truth, for all healing is divine, and our doctors are placed in this society as healers; our psychiatrists are placed here as healers; every nurse is a healer. Everyone who has dedicated his or her life to the ministry of healing is in co-operation and in complete line and parallels what we are doing in the healing ministry of the church. We are always very careful as we talk about the Biblical basis of healing to stress this as a principle understanding on the part of those who are going to introduce themselves to this subject. I have never known a physician, be he agnostic or not, who does not believe and will not tell you that 60 to 70% of the people who come to him today are not physically ill. They are emotionally ill. They have one kind of frustration or another. And how many physicians will say, "It is the job of you fellows to get the lives of these people rooted in something that is important, so that at the first pain, they do not believe they have cancer." How many of us really have a dread of certain diseases simply because we haven't the faith enough to eliminate this fear? How many of us imagine we have all sorts of dreadful diseases at the first instance of illness? "A healthy mind makes a healthy body."

To be sure one ought not to be glib about this because of the frightening things that come to our lives day by day in this whole matter of sickness. But from the viewpoint of the Bible we have clear instruction on how to handle this, as you will note as we proceed.

### *Divine Intervention*

There are three notable ways by which God reaches us about human affairs in the area of healing, in other words, divine intervention.

## Biblical Background

## *1- THE TEN COMMANDMENTS*°

"Thou shalt have no other gods before me."
"Thou shalt not make unto thee any graven image."
"Thou shalt not take the name of the Lord thy God in vain."
"Remember the sabbath day, to keep it holy."
"Honor thy father and thy mother."
"Thou shalt not kill."
"Thou shalt not commit adultery."
"Thou shalt not steal."
"Thou shalt not bear false witness against thy neighbor."
"Thou shalt not covet any thing that is thy neighbor's."

First of all the Bible instructs through the law. Seeing man's disobedience as a tragedy, God apparently thought to help him into obedience again by setting up a system of rules. This we understand in theology and philosophy as the moral law of life. We see it clearly in the Ten Commandments. Within this decalogue is embodied the rules pertaining to our association with God, and the last six pertain to our wholesomeness in regard to one's fellowmen. It has been said that had it been possible for man to obey these commandments and were possible in the world of today, we would have wholeness.

"Thou shalt have no other gods before me. Thou shalt not make unto thee any graven image. Thou shalt not take the name of the Lord thy God in vain." These are three tremendous commandments. If you and I have no other gods, our mind is then primarily set on Him, and if we allow nothing in the world to come in to intervene and interfere between our mind and God's mind, then it would necessarily follow that

---
° Exodus 20

we would be completely God's, wouldn't it? If we would not intervene by taking God's name in vain or we would have no kind of question in our mind who is supreme and sovereign in our lives, we would then be well ordered. You can see this in the generation gap which we have today. (And I am interested in that gap because I am a part it myself.) Unfortunately, each of us, no matter what his age may be, is part of this generation gap. We may be young, or may be older. What is the one thing that bothers most youngsters about their parents? It is that they cannot understand what parents mean when they talk from the frame of reference of experience. Isn't it strange that one of the commandments deals with that very thing? "Honor thy father and thy mother, that thy days may belong in the land which the Lord thy God giveth thee." Honor! Respect! The experience that you may live long enough in the land, that you may also have experience, that you may pass it on to others who will be behind you in this line of humanity.

This year in speaking to from three to five thousand high school seniors at commencement addresses, given in the midst of college riots, one of the things I said was this. "Don't try to put an old head on young shoulders. When you get to college, trust the administration to know more about running the university than you do. Trust your professors to have the experience to impart to you the knowledge which they have accumulated through the years. If you are to be a scholar, be patient enough and decisive enough to be able to sift what you will need for the rest of your life. If you begin to riot, you upset your equilibrium emotionally and intellectually, and out of it, all you will get is a sick person."

## BIBLICAL BACKGROUND

"There will come a time when you have a right to object to authority. The time will come when by your experience, you will have the authority to challenge authority. But do not, until you are there, expect serious-minded and well-educated people to give much notice to your cry for freedom because all of us have gone through the same thing. We have all revolted and rebelled, and we have been this way before. Wait until you have the wisdom to challenge authority and then challenge it with all your might. 'Honor thy father and thy mother.' "

All of these commandments, each in his own way, has a message in the Spiritual Healing area. "Remember the Sabbath Day to keep it holy." I do not know what your opinion may be, and I hope you will not think me too conservative if I say to you that I think a great deal of the problems with humanity today and reasons for so many tranquilizers is because we don't take one day out of seven to rest. We go seven days "pell mell" just as hard and fast as we can. There was a plan given to us: "Six days thou labor and do all thy work, but the seventh is the day of the Lord thy God."° It was set up for two things, as I see it. One is worship; the other is rest. I am not able to dictate nor evaluate for you what is rest, but I am surely not far off when I say that I doubt 36 holes of golf played on Sunday is rest for the man who is trying to find recreation from his office or business. Now, I love golf; I love boating; I love bicycling. I do all of these things but try to do them in order. I try to do them in relation to the other things which are in my life, and I am quite sure there would be people in my congregation who,

---
° Exodus 20:9

when they see me riding a bicycle on the street, think, "Well, he should be out making calls rather than riding a bicycle." But, you see, I have spanned my life to last a long time and have planned my ministry to go over a long period of time. A part of it is being spent in the church that I serve. In order for anyone to serve to his capacity, he must be careful of his health, and you and I must take time to acknowledge that God in our lives has commanded us to look at the long spell, and not simply "burn ourselves out" as a candle, by driving and pushing ourselves or by thinking, "Well, the devil never takes a vacation." I had a minister say that to me one time. He also said, "I've never taken a vacation all of my life." One day he died. Then the church went on vacation, and had great problems and difficulties for a long while afterward. Because this man thought he was so valuable to that congregation that he couldn't take a vacation, the congregation ended up losing because for so long a time they have believed that no one else but he could stand in that pulpit, and never had a chance to find out otherwise. No one else could preside at their funerals and burials, could marry their daughters, or baptize their children. A great man he was, but there is a certain danger in that kind of ministry.

Let me pose a question as far as health is concerned. Do you think a strict adherence to the law will have anything to do with health? It's a good question because it comes to us in the Bible in many different ways. Let us apply it to the present. Take the civil law with which you and I live. You go through a red traffic light sometime and then answer the question for me . . . . especially if you're hit going through. Do you believe that over-eating has anything to do with

## BIBLICAL BACKGROUND

health? There is a law about temperance in this whole matter. I don't know about you, but I find that I have to discipline myself to leave off some of that wonderful food.

The law has great effect on health discipline. It has a great effect on health, physical, mental, and spiritual. If we discipline ourselves in the area of thought, we will always have the chance of strong mental health. How many of you men can see some of yourself in the following? As you get up in the morning and get out the razor to shave, you look in the mirror and begin at once to put up in front of you, straw men. Which of these could be you?

"That so and so is a pain in the neck! If he as much as looks sideways at me today, I'm really going to let him have it."

"The President of the Board has a grudge against me."

"The Vice President is a yes-man, and he better not go sticking his nose in my business today."

"The boss bothers me, and I sure hope I don't run in to him today."

"That guy doesn't do any work. I do 10 times more than he does."

By the time you leave the mirror, you have got a real straw man built up here. When you get to work and meet that fellow, he greets you with a very cheery hello and pats you on the back and says, "That was a great job you did the other day. I don't know what we'd ever do without you in this organization." And there you stand, thinking, "What in the world was I thinking about this morning?" You see, the law of kindness, of generosity, of compassion, of empathy, of positive thought effects your health and mind in a very real sense.

## Spiritual Healing

If we were able to strictly abide by the rules of life, we would always have a sense of well-being in our relationship with others and with God. If we were obedient to the law of the commandments, we would be completely free from guilt as far as the moral and spiritual is concerned. Who has not questioned himself at one time or another about the temptation they felt concerning the last six commandments? "Thou shalt not bear false witness against thy neighbor." "Thou shalt not covet anything which is thy neighbors." Can you truthfully say to yourself that you have never coveted? These catch us in one way or another, but the intention of the rules of God as they were given were given that we might be brought into wholeness.

## 2- PROPHETS

The second area of Biblical truth in the matter of healing comes to us through the prophets. God next sought to bring mankind into an understanding of his position upon the breach of the law. He sought next to bring the truth through the great prophets of the Old Testament. In this great section is the record of God seeking through the tongue of those whom he had inspired to point the way to Israel to health, that they might be saved. It's an amazing area in the Bible if you will only study it to see how much the prophets deal and how many of their sayings deal with the element of being healed. Look through at just the headings of the various chapters and see the many, many acts of healing that took place.

One passage deals with the saving of Israel, and Israel becoming whole. "Comfort ye, comfort ye, my people, saith your God. Speak ye comfortably to

## BIBLICAL BACKGROUND

Jerusalem, and cry unto her, that her warfare is accomplished, that her iniquity is pardoned: for she hath received of the Lord's hand double for all her sins."° "But He was wounded for our transgressions, He was bruised for our iniquities: the chastisement of our peace was upon Him; and with His stripes we are healed."° It would be a mistake if we kept out of the wisdom literature of the Old Testament as well. In Proverbs are these words, which incidentally are comprehensive instructions on the healing ministry. "Attend to my words; incline thine ears unto my sayings. Let them not depart from thine eyes; keep them in the midst of thine heart. For they are life unto those that find them, and health to all their flesh."° This passage calls attention to three essential things which must always be present in healing and its relation to God's word. There must always be an attentive ear, a steadfast look, and an enshrining heart.

Our eyes are on our symptoms more than on God's promises. We have seeds of doubt sewn in our spiritual earth. Our symptoms many times may point to death, but God's word always points to life. Remember that.

Again and again I am asked questions by people who are in the hospital or those with relatives who are seriously ill. "The doctor says there is nothing more that we can do. I guess we'll just have to give up." Almost always accompanying this statement is "I guess we'll have to abide by God's will." I used to let that slide over, but no longer do I let it pass. God's will? I say, "Do you really want to abide; do you mean

---
° Isaiah 40
° Isaiah 53:5
° Proverbs 4:20-22

what you say? I guess now we'll have to abide by God's will? What is God's will? Is it God's will that your child should die? Is it God's will that this person now be taken from this life?" God's will is for wholeness. God's will is for this person to be perfect. Now what are we going to believe in?

Again and again we find that accidental thing being said, blaming God because it is an easy assumption, easy excuse when we can think of nothing else to say, "Well, it must have been God's will." And how I think God must be really disturbed again and again when we say that. How He must really grieve when He hears us say in a kind of negative affirmation, "Well, there's nothing else we can do so we'll let God be responsible for the death of this person."

No, God's will is for life. We must learn also that life is not always physical and temporal and material. We must learn that sometimes God's perfect will is allowing or permitting what takes place here so that the overarching purpose of God's will, life itself, may **come in that eternal manner.**

This is pointed out clearly for us in the experience of Simon Peter on the lake.° Jesus is walking on the water, and Peter, seeing him from the boat, says, "If that's you, Lord, I'm going to get out and walk on the water too. Bid me come to you." Jesus said, "Come," and Peter got out of the boat. As long as the stimulus was on the Lord, Peter got along fine, but you will remember that Peter took his mind off the Lord and put it on the waves. He sank. There is a lesson for you. There is always a stimulus and a response set up by our belief and our faith in God, and as long as we keep

---

°Matthew 14:22-23

## BIBLICAL BACKGROUND

the stimulus on God, we are stimulated to do that which He wants us to do and be that which He wants us to be. On the other hand, when we begin to hear the noise of the waves and the storm of the sea, and that becomes more important to us than centralizing on God, we always sink. There is another part to this story, the result. Peter reached out and said, "Lord, save me," and Jesus stretched out his hand and caught him. Jesus said, "Oh you, of little faith, why did you start to doubt and take your mind from me?" And this makes me think of the verse, "Lo, I am with you always, even unto the end of all things." If that promise is good, then you can walk on the water figuratively. When your trouble area comes along, you can wade right through it, for he is always with you.

### 3- *JESUS CHRIST*

There remains a third area in God's word, the area through our Lord Jesus Christ in the New Testament. Remember all along it is God's intention to bring man into a new relationship, a restored relationship, new life in the redemptive community. I am excited to be a minister in the last half of the Twentieth Century. I wouldn't trade places with any of the 18th or 19th Century preachers, as great as they were. I think I am well aware that perhaps we are not as exegetical° as they, and perhaps we are not as orthodox as they were in their theology, but I wouldn't trade places with any other generation in the world. If you're a good churchman, I want to tell you that there was never a more exciting time to be a member of Christ's Church than right now. Tremendous things are taking place in

---

°exegesis .... a critical explanation of a portion of Scripture

the life of the church, and any of you who are pondering a little and wondering whether or not you're going to stay by it, you just leave it, and in five years from now, you'll be the sorriest soul in the world and come crawling back with a very shamed face trying to get back on the rolls of the church because it is such an exciting and tremendous adventure.

The reason for this is that this is precisely what our Lord promised. There would be days of crisis. There would be days when we would be tested. Do you remember that very famous passage in Revelation? "He that endureth to the end, the same shall be saved." It is the enduring quality that Christ introduces to us, the healing ministry of His miracles. Let me put his miracles of healing to you as is so well recorded in Bernard Martin's book *The Healing Ministry in The Church.*

*Individual healings by Jesus are recorded in the Gospels 48 times. The healings of large numbers of people are recorded in the Gospels 18 times. The general statements on Christ as a healer occur 4 times in the Gospel. And Christ heals through his disciples. There are three passages of sending out of the twelve°, and one on the sending out of the seventy°. The disciples record numerous individual healings and collective healing, i.e. more than one but not a multitude.* It is not surprising from such a cursory view to believe that the Gospels are intent on presenting something that you and I may have overlooked.

It is not a mistake that the Acts of the Apostles, in recording the history of the early church, had the significant intention to say to all who would read there-

---

° Matthew 10:1, 5   Mark 6:7-11   Luke 9:1-5
° Luke 10:1

## BIBLICAL BACKGROUND

after that an important facet of the life of this first Christian Century has been in the healing ministry. Those who are to believe in Christ will take careful note, and those who are to follow Christ and His ambassadors will take very careful attention that in the church of the Twentieth Century the power returns to that church when it comes as near obeying God's word as it possibly can interpret that word for the time in which it finds itself.

In reflection upon the Church of Jesus Christ in the nineteen hundred years of its history, we need make no apology whatsoever because of the preaching and teaching ministry of that church, and I say this without equivocation. As I look across the history of the Church, I am proud of the church as the custodian of the truth of the Gospel. I say to you unflinchingly that the Church has a record no other institution can claim. No other institution can in any sense be paralleled in what its commission was to do in the world. The Church has faithfully fulfilled that commission as far as preaching and teaching is concerned. ("Go preach, go teach, go heal.")

In the third area ("Go heal."), we do not lay claim to much pride. For it is a truth that we have neglected the area of healing in the life of the Church. This has not been done so much by intent, I think, as it has by misunderstanding. It has been done quite frequently from the viewpoint of lack of knowledge, for it was in 325 A.D. that the Council of Nicea was called together for the historical purpose of determining what is the Person of Christ. Here is an interesting point. Whenever the Church has gotten into argument about who Jesus is, it has always lost its power. When the Church has accepted Christ as the Divine intervention, as the Word made flesh come to dwell among us, and when the Church in any period of its history has let Jesus Christ be the living God, that Church in that period has always been distinctive and has always ministered greatly to its age. That is why it is such an exciting thing to be a part of the Twentieth Century Church, for we are making a great rediscovery that the Holy Spirit is not something which is an idea, but the Holy Spirit is a living reality, a living force, a living power in the life of the Church and in the life of the individuals who lay claim to the promise "You shall do wonderful things when the Holy Spirit is come upon you."

In these latter days of this Twentieth Century the Holy Spirit of God is falling upon the Church in this healing ministry in a most powerful and dynamic way. Do not miss the blessing of exposing yourself to the Spirit of God in the healing ministry. If you are in need, then believe that He will heal you, and it will be done. "Therefore I say unto you, What things soever ye desire, when ye pray, believe that ye receive them, and ye shall have them."°

If you know of others who are in want, do not be afraid as a committed Christian to invite them into an experience of the laying on of hands, because in this way you and I are ambassadors. This is not a matter of clergy, or a matter of those who are ordained. We do not have any particular ordination to the healing ministry of the Church. You are all ordained to this when you become a part of Christ, when He becomes a part of you. At that moment you believe His promises, you become an instrument in His hand. No clergyman is a healer. God is always the healer. For

°Mark 11:24

## BIBLICAL BACKGROUND

any person to lay claim to the idea that he is a healer is to lay claim to something that can very well be misunderstood and is a stretch of the truth. For all of you, if you are God's, are called to do God's work. In the anointing and the laying on of hands, you, as a committed Christian, can be a part in this holy ministry. Therefore, when someone comes to you and needs your help, do not turn aside, but in God's name and in faith believing, do what you can. I tell you, you will be amazed at the wonder of God's grace as He uses you to administer His healing power in helping others to find that wholeness He has promised.

"Hate begets hate, violence engenders violence, hypocrisy is answered by hypocrisy, war generates war and love creates love."
(P.A. Sorokin, *The Ways and Power of Love*)


"Finally, be ye all of one mind, having compassion one of another, love as brethren."
(I Peter 3:8)


"Beloved, let us love one another: for love is of God; and everyone that loveth is born of God, and knoweth God."
(I John 4:8)

"This is my commandment, That ye love one another, as I have loved you. Greater love hath no man than this, that a man lay down his life for his friends."
(John 15:12)

"God is love."
(I John 4:8)

"Divine Love always has met and always will meet every human need."
(Mary Baker Eddy)

"For all law is fulfilled in one word, even in this; thou shalt love thy neighbour as thy self."
(Galatians 5:14)

# 4

## The One Word Which Heals

"Drop thy still dew of quietness
Till all our strivings cease.
Take from our souls the strain and stress
And let our ordered lives confess
Thy beauty of thy peace.
Were this whole realm of nature mine
That were a present far too small.
Love so amazing, so divine,
Demands my life, my soul, my all."

SOMETIMES IT IS very difficult for us to relinquish the past, to remind ourselves that we are a part of the future. This is especially true when we read some of the modern versions of Scripture. Some of us have become so thoroughly rooted and love the King James version that we can't really understand the modern translations.

## Spiritual Healing

"I may be able to speak the languages of men and even of angels, but if I have not love, my speech is no more than a noisy gong or a clanging bell. I may have the gift of inspired preaching, I may have all knowledge and understand all secrets, I may have all the faith needed to move mountains, but if I have not love, I am nothing. I may give away everything I have and even give up my body to be burned, but if I have not love, it does me no good. Love is patient and kind; love is not jealous or conceited or proud; love is not ill-mannered or selfish or irritable; love does not keep a record of wrongs; love is not happy with evil but is happy with truth; love never gives up; its hope, faith and patience never fail. Love is eternal. There are inspired messages, but they are temporary. There are gifts of speaking, but they will cease. There is knowledge, but it will pass, for our gifts of knowledge and of inspired messages are only partial, but when what is perfect comes, then what is partial disappears. When I was a child, my speech, feeling, and thinking were all of a child; now that I am a man I have no more use for childish ways. What we see now is like the dim image in a mirror. Then we shall see face to face. What I know now is only partial; then it will be complete, as complete as God's knowledge of me. Meanwhile these three remain .... faith, hope, and love. These three remain, and the greatest of these is love, the one word which heals."\*

If you would be able to understand love and put it into practice, you would know exactly what it is I am going to talk about. Some years ago at the beginning of the war in Viet Nam, one of the St. Louis papers in

---

\* I Corinthians 13

## The One Word

an evening edition carried a remarkable picture. It had been planned beforehand on the return of the first officer of the St. Louis district coming home because of an injury in Viet Nam. His leg had been shot off. It seemed to be a good human interest story, so the photographer and the reporter went out to the airport. There was the young wife and two small children, waiting to meet the plane. The rest of the crowd was not permitted, as usual, to go onto the ramp, but the young wife with her two children was allowed, along with the press, to go out to the foot of the stairs to greet this young hero as he came off the plane. Apparently by some pre-arrangement, the crowd on the plane had planned that the young officer should come off first. When the door opened and the stairs put in place, here came the young officer with a crutch, hobbling down the steps very slowly into the arms of his waiting wife at the bottom. There, as their arms entwined and the tears were shed, the crutch suddenly fell from under his arm and toppled to the ground. An imaginative reporter put this caption under the picture, "The crutch isn't needed here." The one word which heals . . . . love. In this particular incident the young wife became completely unconscious of the lost limb, and the young officer became completely unconscious of the crutch. Gathered together in that singular moment of love, they were caught up and enraptured by the one thing which heals.

If the Church of Jesus Christ is ever to make any kind of contribution in the last half of the Twentieth Century, it must discover the full impact and centrality of meaning which lies in that word love. It is not enough, you see, for us to say, "The poor you have with you always." It is not enough to say that these people who are different from us in race and color and creed should have their rights. It is not enough for us to be fractious in our own comfort and in our own conservatism and to decide that others get along the best way they can. If the church is to make any sort of contribution, it will do it through the one word that heals. At the heart of the healing ministry of the church must come this word of God. If you and I do not understand this in our own person, in our relationships in the society of which we are a part, then everything about the Gospel of Christ becomes ineffectual, and all we are in the world non-effective. You see, we are His hands, His feet. We are His message. As He endows us with the great power of the Spirit to be that particular agent, that instrument, that channel through which His purpose flows, certainly it will not flow if it does not flow on the wings of love. "If we love one another, God dwelleth in us, and his love is perfected in us."°

In Paul Carroll's play *Shadow and Substance*, the servant girl for Canon Scarret reveals the canon's contradictory character to the local schoolmaster who hates Canon Scarret. "Oh, I know," says Bridget, "you have the dagger for him because he can hurt and say killing words. You see him when he's proud, but I see him when he's praying in his little place, and the tears are on his cheeks. You see him when he dines, but I see him when he fasts. You see him when his head is up and fiery like a lion; I see his head when it's down low, and his words won't come. It's because of that you hate him, and because of that I love him. If we could all see each other all the time in big hanging mirrors,

---

° I John 4:12

the whole hate of the world would turn to dust."

That is the reason I am so deeply interested in Spiritual Healing. Somehow in this grand and terrible time when the tensions in our society are so strict, the hates and prejudices so italicized, and the wounds of the world so deep and raw, where do men turn in a time like this for any answer? If we do not have the answer, then in God's name we ought to quit pretending that we have.

If we do not have the solutions, we then ought to quit prattling the notion that we have. It seems to me, as I view it more objectively every day, that from the experience of those who have been in deep trouble, those who have had severe wounds, those who have hated others, that in the love of Christ they have found the healing influence of His majestic life. It has changed them so that they are no longer wounded, nor do they any longer wound. They are no longer spiteful, and neither do they hold resentments and prejudices. If I had seen nothing else in the healing ministry of the church in the last eight years except the popular, the socialite, the millionaire change from selfishness to unselfishness, isolation to concern, and self-aggrandizement to a stewardship of life . . . . if I had seen nothing else, I thank God that I have been introduced to it. And if this were all I had seen, I would still admit to you that the healing ministry of the church is the only thing I have seen that has so drastically changed men's lives.

### *The Three Types of Love*

"Love is a many splendored thing!" In the Christian sense we use it in three notable words . . . . Eros, Philios, and Agape.

## Spiritual Healing

### 1- EROS

Love which consumes is that Eros type of love with which we are all born, the wild passion or driving type of love which possesses us and can indeed make fools of us. Without that love, life is only partial. Therefore, we ought not to condemn as Christians the Eros type of love. In the healing sense we ought to capture it and see this dynamic, powerful type of love which, when harvested and put to the proper application in the life of an individual, can have so rich a meaning as to form companionship with the opposite sex in a marriage that elevates the individual to a place of human-ness; this human-ness coming so very near being a symbol of the divine. What is more significant than the love of a man for a maid, or a maid for a man, when it has the full blessing of the theory and the practical application of love at work every moment of that companionship? Blessed are those who in their marriage possess that quality, the Eros quality which is not easily put out.

Some years ago in our church, we had the 50th (Golden) Wedding Anniversary of a couple from our congregation. As I came up to them, because I knew these lovely people so well, I said to Mrs. McMack, "You know, I congratulate you for putting up with Dave for 50 years."

She laughed at this, and Dave also got a kick out of it and said, "Aren't you going to say anything about what I've put up with all these 50 years?"

"You know," I replied, "to me it's a great blessing to be able to stand here and congratulate you on your 50th Wedding Anniversary. Not everyone has this privilege and opportunity."

He then said a touching thing, "There has never been one moment of regret in my life all of the time I

## The One Word

have lived with this girl. I am only sorry that I cannot say that I wish I had another 50 years to live with her."

She, in return, made a priceless statement, "I have loved Dave with such a tremendous love that there were times when I could kill him. But," she continued, "my love was of such an extreme nature that when I wanted to kill him, it only moved me to love him more."

The one word which heals. What a magnificent thing . . . . the Eros type of love when properly understood.

One of the great regrets that I have is that I have so little time to get across to our young marrieds what this type of love can really mean. We are all "fired up" in our youthful days of marriage with the passion, the experimentation of sex, and all of this is good and right, but I have a feeling so many never get to the next plateau. They never fully understand that Eros in the area of devotion, area of sacrifice, and area of answering the needs of others.

As a counselor, again and again, I have the very unsavory and unlovely experience of sitting down with a handsome couple of young people, having the girl say to me, "Whenever he touches me, I go cold." You see, love is a many splendored thing, and the healing influence that comes from our love in the physical is of such worth that here if we understand it perfectly, we understand the true meaning of what God intended in that splendid and magnificent contract of marriage.

### 2- PHILIOS

**We translate the Greek word *Philios* from which we** get the word filial. It is the love which accepts, not the love that consumes. The son and daughter in our family accept our love, and we accept from them in turn their love. I wonder if we really ever understand the meaning of that expression. Sometimes I am quite sure that our children love us because they have a sense that to do anything less is wrong, and this is an accidental feature for a parent to be engaged in that kind of a comradeship, isn't it? If the love which accepts is real, then the love of a child for a parent has great meaning and significance.

## 3- *AGAPE*

Agape is the love that gives. This is the outgoing love, the second mile love, loving when you would rather do something else. Do you understand it? This is the love of God for us in Christ. It is the love which is so expansive, and I doubt very much that we can truly understand it, yet once in a while one sees it in the human venture.

At Princeton Theological Seminary some years ago when asked by our General Assembly to be on a team of seven examining, I was teamed with a very wonderful layman from Baltimore. A great man he was, and we had three of the nine Seminaries of our church, Princeton being one of them. John McKay was still president of Princeton at this time, and I shall never forget the cold winter day as I came into Philadelphia and then took the junction train that went to Dr. McKay's office. He had been an acquaintance of mine for a good number of years, and on this occasion he spent a very busy day with us, showing us everything. In the afternoon at 4:30 we had a faculty meeting in which we had the responsibility of "picking the brains" of the faculty as to what they thought about theological education in the present time, and

# The One Word

what were they doing as professors to try to make the right kind of Presbyterian ministers in this grand and awful time. Well, it was a delightful experience. After such a very long day, at dinner as we were eating in the Commons, John McKay said to us, "Now, if there's anything else you want to see, do not hesitate to stay as long tonight as you wish. We have rooms for you overnight. I will have to get away before too long because I'm leaving for Africa tomorrow morning."

"Dr. McKay," I replied, "why didn't you tell us? You spent all day with us, and it wasn't necessary at all for you to do this. I know we've robbed you of some very wonderful hours with your wife and family before you leave, and I apologize."

And in his inimitable Scot way he held up his hand and said, "George, if I thought you'd take it that way, I never would have mentioned it at all. It's my business to be with you."

Both Ted and I tried to say to him that he should go immediately and go home to get ready. He was to be gone for three months and spending all this time with us. Ted had driven his own car from Baltimore and so bade us goodbye. I said to Dr. McKay, "If you will just help me find a cab, I'll go down to the station."

As I reached out my hand, he said, "No, I'm going with you."

"Oh," I replied, "John, please, you're embarrassing me. Now go home and spend these last few hours with Mrs. McKay."

"No, I'm going with you. There are some things I want to talk over about our Seminaries."

We sat in the little junction station waiting for the train to pull out. We had about a half hour together, one of the most precious half hours of my life, as John

McKay let me into his heart in a very warm and wonderful way. He told me about some of the hard days when he was so severely criticized by some in our church because of his stand on certain issues in theological education. As soon as the conductor came and said we could board now for Philadelphia, I immediately got up and, knowing that if I got on the train, John would leave, bade him goodbye. I was the only passenger and sat for about four minutes, and as I looked out the window quite by accident, there was John McKay still standing on the platform. As the train pulled out, John took off his hat and waved goodbye with it. A man whose love of his fellowman, whose Agape, was so sensitive that he was completely unselfish. His thought of Africa and going to Africa meant nothing until his guests were properly ushered out of Princeton. Are you that good a host? How many fellows I've taken to the airport and quickly bade them goodbye. How many I have put on the train and left the platform. Agape, the love that is so out-going that it ministers in unforgettable ways. The touch of the Master's hand through you and through me as His agents of reconciliation, as His agents of peace and mercy and grace in this kind of a world.

### *Loving Hands*

Our hands are a symbol of our expression of love. We have in the healing ministry of the church the laying on of hands. There is an interesting study to make sometime if you will do it. Begin at the beginning of Genesis and go through to Revelation and see how many references there are in Scripture to the laying on of hands or the use of hands. Our hands are really expressive. Have you ever noticed a person's hands?

## The One Word

They tell much about the character of an individual. Be conscious of other people's hands from now on.

Have you ever noticed how some people shake hands with you? After it's all over, you have the feeling that you have not been healed. With others, when they shake hands with you, you feel that you would like to keep your hand there for a long time. There is something comfortable and warm and wonderful about the handshake of certain people. All their love and warmth seems to express itself to you by the touch of the hand. The ministry of healing that comes through a handshake. Be conscious the next time, as a Christian, of the person when you put out your hand. Make it meaningful. Express your inner love and the "Agape" of your spirit in that handshake.

Those of you who are mothers, I need not say to you, the blessing of a mother's hand upon the fevered brow of a child when he or she is ill. You remember, don't you? You would go over to their crib and simply touch them, pat them softly on the back, and immediately, magically, there came a quietness, and the restlessness stopped. Even sometimes in delirium the child would be quieted as you would take that child in your arms. The healing influence and ministry is in a mother's hand.

How many of you who are doctors are conscious of what it means when you touch a patient? You have no idea how much we depend on you, and how many of my people will say as I go to call on them in some moment of illness, "Well, the doctor was in today, and I feel much better."

"Well, what did he do for you?" I would ask.

"Oh, nothing, he was just in. He just stopped to say hello, and he just patted me on the shoulder, and you know, that's better than all the medicine in the world."

Have you ever said that or heard another say it? The truth of it is that in the doctor's hands there is healing, for he has dedicated his life to this ministry of healing. The doctor who has the empathy and patient relationship and really loves people with the Agape type of love is a doctor who can't be stopped in this generation.

I wish I had the chance to lecture to medical schools. So many of our doctors get off into specialization quickly. I wish I could convince some of the young doctors to stay as general practitioners. What a magnificent opportunity they have to treat everything all up and down the gamut of human illness, but the greatest advantage they have over a specialist is they get to know the family. They get to know the whole secret in the use of a stethoscope. The doctor's touch is very important in the use of the blood pressure instrument, for the touch of the hand is very important. And nurses, there is no one who deals with sick people, who touches patients, more than a nurse with her hand. Let it be a healing hand. Or the teacher's or the pastor's hand.

I remember when I was in Seminary, Dr. Farmer, an exquisite man, gave us a lecture one afternoon in the field of homiletics° on the use of your hands. I had no idea that some thirty years later I would see the practicality of his address. He said, "Boys, your hands are very expressive of God's love in you. If you love God, then it's got to come out in two places in you .... in your hands and in your face. I can tell in five

---

° Homiletics—the art of preaching; that branch of theology dealing with sermons

minutes when I'm talking with a clergyman whether he really loves God." I'm not quite as keen as Dr. Farmer, but I think he has something here. In the pastor's hands and in his face is the revelation of what he is. Is there the glow of the Master in your countenance that other people who are looking may see Him there? Is there the touch of the Master's hand in your hand? As other people who are lonely and bereft need the touch, do they receive it from your hand?

## *Healing Through Love*
All healing comes through love, doesn't it? Would you say that all healing comes through God? Then if "God is love," we can conclude that all healing comes through love. There are many agents of this healing love that I think it practical to look at.

## *1- HOME*
I think healing begins in the home. It begins on the night a young man and young woman are married. Healing begins at that point, for the love which they possess for each other will continue through all the years God gives them the grace to live with each other, if they will only remember that they are channels of God's healing influence upon the life of the other.

Those of you who are blessed with wonderful mates, you know what I am talking about . . . . this kind of healing influence. I say to couples that I marry when I counsel them: "You know we often say marriage is a 50-50 proposition, but it is not that. It cannot be that." As I look at Jane and John, I say, "John, Jane will not always have her 50%. She can't possibly have it. Some night you're going to come home and find Jane has burned the beans, and she will be there with only 10%.

Now, John, you've got to be there with the 90%. You see, it's got to be on a ratio." And I usually say, "John, now you go and get Jane's coat and say to her, 'Honey, let's go down town and eat tonight. I'll buy you a filet mignon.' And then see how quickly those tears will dry up."

To Jane I then say, "Jane, sometime John is going to come home from his work, and things won't have gone well that day, and his old chin will be dragging the carpet. He'll be there with the 20%, and now, Jane, you've got to be there with the 80%."

If we are not willing to have that healing influence one with the other, then we miss this whole idea that "love is a many splendored thing." I think it is very difficult to be a clergyman's wife, and I am glad that God did not make me a woman because I probably would have married one. No matter how much sympathy I have for the minister's wife, many of the greatest things that have come in my life have come through my wife in her healing influence upon my spirit, upon my person.

We sometimes have, and must understand, this geriatric problem in our homes. Many of us are in the area where we must consider our aged parents. All of us who are clergymen have again and again this sad problem of going to rest homes, calling upon aged people who have been put there by their families because they didn't want to take care of them. I have a great amount of sympathy for this, and I think one ought never be glib about this at all. One never knows all of the conditions and all of the situations in which one is caught up. I often see older men and women just crying for someone's attention They are alone. It isn't that there is anything wrong with them, other than just pure loneliness. No one takes the time. The sons and daughters are too busy to come to see them, and they have a way of safeguarding the grandchildren so that they don't have to go and see them. Here are these people, and the minute that you go to see them, they say, "Please, sit down and just talk to me. Tell me what is going on downtown, will you?" I call on a man up at The House of Loreto, and all he wants me to tell him is what is going on downtown. When he was active, he always visited the stock market. Now, he must know that I don't visit the stock market, but he wants to know again and again what's going on over on the corner. It happens that one of the fellows who belongs to my Friday morning prayer group is a broker for this particular agency, so I ask him again and again what's going on. I then relate it to my elderly friend, and he thinks I must be doing pretty good in the market. I give him the advice that my friend gives me. I told my broker friend about him one day, and he went up to see him and had a tremendous time. Healing begins in the home. If it is possible for you to take care of your aged loved ones, do it. If it is not possible for you, I would not tell you it was your responsibility, but for the sake of the healing that comes through the home, do it, and you will be blessed by it.

## 2- NEIGHBORHOOD

I think we must look into the healing that comes through love in our neighborhood. Who are your neighbors? It has been our privilege, Hazel's and mine, for most of the time we have lived in our city, now 30 years, to be neighbors with Jewish people. For 10 years our very closest neighbor was a Jewish lawyer and his wife. They had three children; we had two. I shall never forget on one of the feast days when we were invited to their house. The father, as we all stood up behind the table, gave his prayer. The Rabbi and his wife were present, and as we sat down, my friend asked his Rabbi, "Rabbi, would you object if I would ask Dr. Parkinson to say grace on this festival?"

The Rabbi, one of my closest clergy friends, said, "I was hoping you would do that. I would be delighted."

We all took hands, our families. I think I could say to you, I don't believe I was ever any closer to the throne of God than I was on that occasion . . . . the healing influence that comes in a neighborhood. You see, if we are really Christian, we then must love with an immeasurable love those people with whom our Lord Jesus Christ associated as family.

Whenever I find anybody who is raucous and prejudiced, I always wonder about the healing element of love at work in the neighborhood. Sometime in your neighborhood you are going to have the high privilege of having a Negro move into your community. This may threaten some people, but you may expect it in your neighborhood. How are you going to react to it? Are you enough of a follower of Christ that you, through your love, can minister in a healing way in that neighborhood, or will the "For Sale" sign go on your front yard?

> "Were this whole realm of nature mine
> That were a present far too small
> Love so amazing, so divine
> Demands my soul, my life, my all."

They are easy words to repeat. They are not easy words to enact. Here is the answer to our race problem . . . . not riots, not the burning of buildings and communities, but love let loose, the love of God let loose upon the community and in the hearts of men to such an extent that we are willing to give all. From it the healing influence of the spirit of God becomes a reality.

## 3- *CHURCH*

I turn to the healing that must take place within the church. All of us who have had any experience in working in national areas or working with ministers over a broad scale testify to the fact that probably no day in the history of the church do we have more pastors with broken hearts than we do today.

One of the saddest commentaries on the life of the church is the number of pastors who are restless and would rather move. If I am talking to any of you, may I say this to you. Don't move if you can help it. Don't move, because you'll find the same problems wherever you move. The same people will be in the new parish. Just love the people where you are. Love them with such an out-going love even to the place where you have to apologize. There ought never be anything wrong with a minister apologizing to a layman. We are human beings. If we are nettled sometimes and show our temper, that indicates our normalcy. If I were a trustee, I'd raise that minister's salary, because I would know that he is a human being, and we have some chance of making something out of him. You see, a fellow who never gets angry, never shows any temper, is always placid, and never shows any humaneness at all, I don't believe he could preach to me on Sunday morning because I would be convinced that he lived entirely in an "ivory tower." I do not want to listen to someone who lives in an ivory tower; I want to know someone who gets his knuckles rubbed raw and fingernails dirty at work in the hard inner city, in the hard core where things are taking place and where it's dangerous to stand up and be counted as a soldier of Christ.

I know many members with broken hearts because of pastors. Not too long ago a man from a neighboring community came to me and said he wanted to transfer his letter to our congregation because of an incident that had happened. I think I talked him out of it. My reason for talking him out of it was because I thought he needed to do something for his pastor. This is what had urged him to transfer.

His wife's father had died in Arizona, and he went over to his pastor, living just across the street, to say, "Before my wife leaves, would you, please, come over and have a prayer with her?"

I couldn't believe it, and can only take his word for it, but he related that the minister replied, "I'm afraid I can't make it this afternoon. I've got a golf date."

"Now, you'll be surprised, George," he said, "what I said to that minister, and I apologize to you because I can't apologize to him. I'm too angry. I said," he continued, "*to hell with you.* And I meant it, and I can't go back to that church any more."

"Why of course you can," I told him, "but you've got to apologize to him."

"How can you apologize to a man so insensitive as that?"

"You've got the greatest opportunity in the world to make a minister out of that man by sitting down and letting him see how really hurt you were, and then saying to him at the end, 'Do you mind if we have prayer?' Then *you* pray in an intercessory fashion. Don't pray beating him over the head. Don't pray that

## The One Word

God may show him his mistake, but pray for him in a genuine spirit of healing love until you get across to him that you are not going to leave his church, but you're going to put your arms around him so that the next time he has a chance, he'll not say 'I have a golf date,' but he'll drop his golf bags on the way out and go make that call and that prayer as the first priority of his life."

There's much more that we need say about this. I know that there may be those that feel threatened because you think your church is not doing as a denomination, what you think it ought to do. It's getting itself mixed up in a lot of other things that are to you relatively unimportant. The time has come in this time A.D. when we must see that there is a difference in what is important in the life of the church and what was important fifty years ago. As far as the history of the Christian Church is concerned, we cannot minister in the way we did fifty years ago. This is a new day. This is a new age, demanding a new approach to the Gospel, and the healing ministry is a part of that new approach.

### 4- COMMUNITY

Next we must look at the healing that comes in the community. Should the church be in politics? I'll say it should! It should be there, not to tell people how to vote, but undergirding the whole system of government. When was the last time you called or wrote to your mayor and said to him, "Thank you, Mr. Mayor, for what you did on the referendum regarding the church." Do you know what the mayors of the cities where I go tell me? They listen all of the time to the underworld, to the gamblers, to the law breakers, but I have had mayors say to me almost with a shaking voice, "But we just never hear from the good people. Certainly there are some good people left, yet we never hear about anything good we have done." The healing influence of love in your community is needed here. When your councilman stands up to be counted for something that you have wanted him to do, let him know. It's an easy thing to write your Congressman and your Senator and try to put pressure on them for that which you want to happen, but do you ever think of writing when it is passed, a letter of thanks in return for what they have done? Many will say that most of our representatives don't truly represent their people, but do their people truly represent them? Letting them know the pleasures and assurances as well as the complaints are what creates a working team.

The Congressman of the 16th Ohio District is a member of my congregation. Frank Bow is the ranking Republican member on the Appropriations Committee in the House of Representatives. Mr. Bow tells me, "I get floods of letters, telegrams, telephone messages, all kind of propaganda insisting that I do this and do that and the other, but, George, when we get it done, we never hear a word of thanks. Nobody ever takes the time then to say 'thank you.'"

And I replied, "Frank, they say 'thank you' at the polls. That's when they say their thanks."

"But," he said, "It's such a lonely life, such a lonely life."

You and I could be a part of the healing of the community if we would only take part and do it.

## The One Word

### 5- CONCLUSIONS

I will not take the time, for you know the aim at which I am arriving. The agents of healing through love are the home, the neighborhood, the church, the community, and carries to the healing love in the nation, and finally the healing in the world. I don't have much faith in peace negotiations today. I say that not because of any pessimism, because I am an optimist, but only because I think we are aiming at the wrong thing. We're in a chess game. We are saying to the North Vietnamese, "You cease your particular warfare, and we will stop our bombing." They reply, "You stop bombing in the north, and we'll stop our aggression." That is a chess game . . . . a stalemate.° Somebody, sometime, is going to have to make a move. America has been known in history at least as a Christian nation. Would you believe with me that there are enough Christian people in this United States of America who can really pray that we might act like a Christian nation and take the risk and make the attempt to put the healing hand of love on this very tense situation and in faith believe that God would do His work of healing among the nations? Who knows but what in the history of civilization, this is our grandest hour. Who knows but what in this moment, this is our destiny. Help us, each of us, to be able to find in our hearts the possibility of letting that one word LOVE so work that we could be a part of the healing influence upon the world.

---

° stalemate—In chess, a deadlock, a standstill

"Cast thy burden upon the Lord, and he shall sustain thee: he shall never suffer the righteous to be moved."

(Psalms 55:22)

# 5

## *The Three D's of Healing*

The healing of His seamless dress,
Is by our beds of pain;
We touch Him in life's throng and press,
And we are whole again.

O Master, let me walk with Thee
In lowly paths of service free;
Tell me Thy secret; help me bear
The strain of toil, the fret of care.

WE TALK ABOUT our burdens, and Spiritual Healing, of course, deals with the very subject of man's burdens. It deals with releasing oneself from the burden that derives from and keeps one enthralled in the mental, spiritual, and physical. There is a very familiar story about the man who was walking down the road, heavily bowed over with the burdens he was carrying. There came along a man in a wagon and said, "My brother, get up and ride with me. You don't need to carry that burden in that way." The man got up on the seat beside the driver, but he still carried the burden on his back. He didn't put it in the back of the wagon. Finally the driver said to him, "Why do you still carry your burden?" The man answered, "Well, you're so good to pick me up, I wouldn't want you to carry my burden also."

We see God in exactly that way so many times. He comes along, and, in a figure of speech, He is the driver, and He says, "My child, get up and ride with me. Be free from your burden." But we still allow ourselves to be bowed over in the seat next to God, and then He says to us, "Why don't you let go of your burden?" We say in reply, "Oh, we wouldn't want to do that to you, Lord. It's enough for us just to ride by You, just to be close to You. We wouldn't ask You to carry our burden also." Of course, the very thing that God has said to us is "Let me have your burden."

In this we have another truism of the Spiritual Healing field, and that is very frequently we carry our burdens to the Lord. We're all good at that. Those of us who are believers, again and again, we go to the Lord with our burdens. But when we leave, we carry them away, and He has said, "Leave your burdens with me." If we do not leave it there, the Lord cannot do anything for us. If we are going to be "burden-toters," there is nothing He can do. This is a man-sided and a God-sided proposition, and our responsibility in this partnership is to trust; God's part in it is to work. He did not tell us to work to unburden ourselves. He only asks that we trust Him when we lay the burden upon Him. "Commit thy way unto the

## The Three D's

Lord; trust also in him; and he shall bring it to pass."*

This may sound like a very selfish type of theology, but the truth of the matter is that this is the only way we can have wholeness. It is impossible for us to do anything for ourselves in the capacity of grace, for grace is a free gift of God. All we can do is claim God's mercy. We have no mercy in ourselves as far as self is concerned, so when we are going to unburden outselves, let's be sure that when we go to the Lord, we leave the burden there and do not keep picking it up again and again and taking it back. This will only cause us the problem which we continually have and causes us to ask questions as to why people do not get help when they pray for it or why do we not find wholeness when we have struggled so desperately for it. One of the answers is, of course, that we do not trust enough the partnership so that the work is done. If I employ a carpenter to build anything for me, I do not expect to employ him and then start hammering on the project. I must trust the carpenter I employ to be able to do the job which I have asked him to do. If I don't trust him, I shouldn't have made any contract with him at all. As blunt as this sounds, this is precisely our arrangement with God. If we do trust God, then we ought not to take back the project from his hands. Once having entrusted it to Him, we ought to have faith and trust that He can accomplish whatsoever we want Him to do.

### 1- *DESIRE*

The first D of Spiritual Healing is *Desire*. If you will note carefully the healings of Jesus, He always asks

---

* Psalms 37:5

about desire of people. In every occasion of the miracles you will discover Jesus never went to the work of laying on of hands on anyone without first of all engaging them in conversation or someone who had brought the person. Jesus always got into touch with the person and the incident in which He was going to work, and He still does this. You and I must do it also.

"What do you want?" He said. "What are you really looking for? Why are you afraid? Why were you embarrassed to touch the hem of my garment? How much faith do you have? Do you really believe?" So we come, asking again and again in the healing ministry, "What do you desire?" A very quick and natural answer to that is "I want to be well." We mean by that, of course, we want to be healthy, so that we can be free from the slavery of disease, and this is an honest desire, one that ought always to be understood by us.

We do not need to condemn anyone who wants to be well. We do not need, in any sense, in the Twentieth Century to feel they are asking an unnatural or an unsavory question. We all want to be well. The reason we want to be well is the very call in our humanity to be normal. Every person alive wants to be normal. What is normal for one may not be normal for another because the law of normality is the law of personality. I never had this so vividly brought to me as I did when I was a student visiting an asylum, which was a field trip for a criminology class. I am sure you will get a chuckle out of this when I tell you I was walking down the hall, and before long I noticed I had a partner, a very lovely middle-aged lady who called herself Josephine. The only problem was is that she called me Napoleon. I sensed very soon, although

## The Three D's

she looked very rational, that she was not normal.

To this woman, however, as was explained to us later by the psychiatrist, we were the ones who were abnormal, and she perfectly normal. She could not understand why I didn't accept my identity, Napoleon. She believed conclusively that she was Josephine, and her whole world was built around that fantasy. The doctor in a very interesting way dealt with her, and as she talked with us, she had an almost perfect analysis of the entire French period in which she lived, in her fantasy, of course.

The thing we are talking about is that we want to be normal. What we mean is that we want to be like the rest of the people who are in our generation and in our society. In other words, we want to get along with other people.

A friend of mine has a very interesting example of this. One day he was driving along this same asylum, and he had something go wrong with his car. He stopped by the road, and by the fence there was a man standing. My friend removed the tire and took it to a filling station. When he brought it back, he had difficulty getting it back on. He couldn't figure out why he had the difficulty. The fellow on the other side of the fence said to him, "If you will only move your car to the level ground, your jack will be on the level, and it will stay in place." My friend said to me, "I began to question in my mind who was right and who was wrong, because this man was supposed to be abnormal, but I was trying to do a very silly thing as far as he was concerned." You see, it depends to a great extent on what is your position from where you take your stand. In the healing ministry of the church we are talking always from the position that a person has the right to be normal. He has the right to expect God to make him healthy. There is no such thing as a notion that you are expecting God to do what He has not promised to do for you.

In this sense we have very good proof from our Lord Himself when he asks repeatedly, "Why do you want to be well?" Here we come to the hard issue of wholeness, for in honesty many of us will answer "That I may play better golf this summer" or "so that I may earn a living" or "so that I just don't feel so tough all the time." But these are all tributaries of wholeness. That is not the real reason a man wants to be whole. The real reason must always be "that I may be able to perform the task which is my life task according to God's will for my life." This is the reason for wholeness, that we may be able to perform the task that God has assigned within His holy will and purpose to the best of our ability.

Notice a few of the incidents of healing in the New Testament, and note the tremendous desire. First of all, the father with the epileptic son.° Jesus had been up on the Mount of Transfiguration with Peter, James, and John, and it has truly been a mountaintop experience, and they came down into the valley and are harshly thrust against the reality of life when the father comes running to Jesus and says, "Can you do anything for my son? If you can, will you do it please?"

"What's going on here?" Jesus asks.

"I came to your disciples," the man replied, "and they have been able to do nothing for him."

And you will remember that our Lord looked upon the occasion with a great degree of concern and asked the father, "Do you believe?"

° Matthew 17:14, Mark 9:14

# The Three D's

What is wrapped up in that question? Was it "Do you believe I can heal your son? Do you believe in God? Do you believe that your son ought to be healed so that he can go about the normal functions of childhood?" What is behind that question "Do you believe?" I think the crucial thing behind it was Jesus was saying to the father, "How great is your desire? How great a significance is your desire." And the father answered, "I do believe, help thou my unbelief." This has been a stickler for exegetes* for a long time. What I think is really being said here is "God knows I have the desire, but I wobble in my belief. I wobble in my belief that things can be different." This is what we find all of the time in the Spiritual Healing Ministry. I doubt very seriously that anyone comes to a healing service, but what they believe. They believe in God. They believe in the Lord Jesus Christ. They believe in the institutional church, the gospel of our Lord, the gospel of salvation, and all the things that are fundamentally the issues of the church. But so many times they wobble on that idea that things can be different.

Those of us who are interested in Spiritual Healing ought to be very patient in that because we have been there and are there so often ourselves. If you had arthritis, for example, in your knees, and you had it for 20 years. It isn't a simple thing to just kneel at a kneeling rail in a church service, have someone lay hands on you, then get up and believe that your arthritis is gone. It isn't easy to believe things can be different. The promise is things *can be* different, depending upon the depth of our desire that we see our-

---
\* exegetes—one skilled in the critical explanation of a portion of Scripture.

selves as whole creatures. Often what we really are praying about is asking God to remove the symptoms rather than the cause, and here is always the problem we are involved in when we are in the Spiritual Healing Ministry.

So when you pray that God will remove the cause, and then you may expect, of course, the symptoms to be delivered. Our doctors know this very well. When they begin to talk with a patient calling on an emergency, they begin first by asking questions. "Tell me about yourself." And then in this particular analysis they begin to develop what is wrong with this person. Often they have to treat the symptoms, it is true, in order to get to the cause. Once they have that patient who is able to tell them "I think my pain comes from this," the doctor can more easily at times see the cause. Frequently there comes a cataclysmic recovery because we are at work in that which is the *root* of the problem.

The father had said in the former incident, "What a wonderful thing it would be to know that my son could be rid of this epilepsy, but I suppose that's too good to be true." Jesus knew all these things were running in the father's mind, and He, of course, said to him, "He can be healed." He went to work and healed the boy. I hope you will not forget that He also healed the father, for this is a double healing. This happens so many times in the healings of our Lord, for not alone was the child healed of his epilepsy, but the father was healed of his lack of trust in the Almighty. His desire, his great desire, brought him into an area of hope and comfort.

Remember the woman with the issue of blood?°

---

° Matthew 9:20, Mark 5:25, Luke 8:43

## The Three D's

There is a great throng in the village, but you will notice her desire if you will read this in the Gospels. She steals out of her house very early in this day, thinking that she can make the village square before the crowd gathers, but as she gets out on the streets, she discovers that she has waited too long. When she gets near to the village square, she finds that the multitude is massed. Let me use my imagination. I think the woman got down on her hands and knees, so she could get through easier. She crawled through and reached out her hand as far as she could reach it. Just as Jesus turned to go away, she made one last desperate reach and touched the hem of his garment, and she was made whole. Jesus said, "What happened here? Something has happened to me?"

And good old Peter replied, "Now, for heaven's sake, Lord, in all this crowd, in all of this multitude you ask 'Who touched me?' Are you serious? Do we really have to find out who for you? Do we really? Why, it's impossible. We can never find out."

Jesus said, "Everyone stop right where you are. There is someone here who has touched me because strength has gone out of me and has gone into that person, and I want to know right now who it is."

The woman by this time was crawling her way back out of the crowd, and she heard this command of our Lord. Because of the magnetism between the power of the spirit of the divine and the human, she, by some strange compulsion, got right up in the middle of that crowd and walked back to Jesus.

Everyone else in the crowd is lost to Him as he relates Himself to this woman, saying, "My dear, you didn't need to be embarrassed. That's why I've come here. I came here that you might be healed. Why would you be afraid? Why would you try to get away? Don't you see, I love you, and I'm here that you may be made whole."

That woman went through her entire life never forgetting that experience. It will be that way with you when you "touch the hem of His garment." In that moment when you are made whole, you will find a new reality and a new thrill, and all of a sudden the Christian life becomes not a drag, but a thrilling adventure. This is what Spiritual Healing is about, to give you the life of Christ as it is intended to be in the lives of those of us who walk after Him.

This is the idea, that we do not embarrass anybody else by our witness. If we are witnessing properly, nobody is ever embarrassed by what we say. They are always uplifted by what we say and comfortable in our presence, and the whole company around us recognizes the strength and power and love that emanates from our personality. Any time you and I make another person want to get away from us because we are witnessing, our witness somehow is wrong. It can be the worst sinner in the world or a person only half committed, but any time we make someone say to himself under his breath, "Oh, brother, what a kook that is. I don't want anything to do with them. Let me get away now just as far as I can." This is not a healthy religion. I cannot find any place in the New Testament where the people want to get away from Jesus. All I find is where they were attracted to Him. Desire on your part and mine helps us to receive the healing touch, so overwhelmingly needed in our day.

## 2- DYNAMIC

The second D is that which I call *dynamic*. It comes

## The Three D's

from a Greek word "Dunamis" meaning power. The word we best know as a derivative of it is the word *dynamite*. What a tremendous word! Think of what Jesus said to His disciples, "Ye shall receive dunamis after the Holy Spirit is come upon you; ye shall be as dynamite." Think of it. Of course, what dynamite means is that it is explosive. It means the rooting up of all of that which is no longer necessary in this particular project. Being strictly honest, it is this thing that we need in our religion today, the dunamis, the power of the Spirit. We know God is not going to heal us of a migraine headache or arthritis and leave us with hate and resentment in our spirit. He will not do it. I can promise you faithfully that when God touches you with His healing hand, it will be a thorough-going healing. It may indeed start in the spirit. It may indeed start imperceptibly, so quietly and unobtrusively that you will not even recognize it. Further than that I can promise you almost faithfully that again and again as you come praying for some particular need, that need may not be answered, but never say that you have never received healing until you begin to really fathom very carefully what is going on in your life. You will discover on many occasions that you pray for one thing, and your healing starts in another area.

Some years ago in one of our healing services, a little lady, a member of the Lutheran Church, attended. She was a little deaf along with having a very serious case of arthritis in her knees. Bless her heart, she was such a lovely person, but being a little deaf, she talked a little too loudly sometimes. One evening after our service, as I was shaking hands with people, she said, "I've been coming here for 6 months and not a thing has happened. Now what do I do?" I could have choked her! There are always people who are there for the first time, and that is not a very good testimony for a healing service, is it?

All I could think to say was, "Keep coming and keep praying, and when God wants to, He'll do it."

I thought that was the best answer I could think of at the time. Some months later, at the healing service I was talking about resentment, and I went at this very seriously and made the same statement that God will not heal you of arthritis and leave resentment in your spirit. She came up to the kneeling rail that evening and went around to the right. She kneeled at the farthest right point, and as I laid hands on her, I knew immediately something had taken place. She got up very gingerly, having had to be helped up the two steps into the Chancel. Now going out, she walked down there just as well as you or I. Underneath my breath, I was praising the Lord for this, and I wondered if she would say anything. After the service, she was about 4 people away from me as we were shaking hands. She couldn't hold it any longer and said, "It happened! It happened! It happened!"

"What happened?" I asked.

"I got my healing! You helped me!" she yelled. "I got my healing when Willard went out of my knees!"

Now who was Willard? Willard was her pastor. So you see, people are dying and suffering today because of simple, unadulterated hate. Some years ago they started to hate someone, and they allowed that to continue and continue and grow and grow until it became an abcess far worse than any cancer could ever be in the physical sense. That hate was literally eating them alive. We see it over and over again, that

## The Three D's

hatred and that bitterness and that envy and that jealousy and that malice, and once it goes, they have a complete healing. And then they will ask, "Why, Why didn't somebody tell me about this before?" As a matter of fact, that's a part of the Gospel.

Nineteen hundred years ago our Lord talked about this very thing. If we are only truthful to that Gospel, we will find the answer . . . . The power of the spirit of God let loose in the life of the world and in each individual, the dynamite that is there to work for us.

### 3- DELIVERANCE

The third D is *Deliverance*. If you won't take no for an answer, you are going to find the blessing of deliverance. I was once conducting a Spiritual Healing Mission in Waverly, Ohio, and met a school teacher there.

Laura was that school teacher, and on this particular summer she had decided to announce to the superintendent that she could not teach school any longer because the arthritis in her hands had developed in such a way that she was in almost continual pain. She had sold her car three months before this time. On a Friday morning at 8 o'clock we had a service. (We always had these at unusual times to draw only those who seriously wanted to come and not those seeking a side-show.) We had an immense number of people in the village come out to this service. I knew nothing about what did happen at that service until some time after. The teacher came to the kneeling rail that morning. A very simple prayer was made with the laying on of hands. While she knelt there, she later told me, this was her prayer. "Lord, I've tried everything in the world, and nothing has worked. Now

## Spiritual Healing

I do believe you can heal me. I'm sick and tired of being this way, and I demand of you that you heal me now. And He did! And He did!"

I heard about this a fortnight after it took place when one of the men who was a part of the group called up and said to me, "You'll be interested to know about Laura, our school teacher down here. She is back teaching school and even went out and bought herself a new Chevy Impala Sports Coupe."

I have ridden in that sports coupe with her driving, and she drives as well as I do, without arthritis in her hands. She always attends our Mission in Canton as her expression of praise and thanks.

If you will not let anyone say no to you, you can be healed. If you will say to God, "I will not take no for an answer," you will be surprised at the tremendous things that God will do for you. If we believe that God wants us to be whole, then we are saying something more than for God to just make us well. I can walk with a limp, if that limp doesn't keep me from being whole. I can get by with an artificial limb, if I can be whole. I don't have to be perfect in any of my compartments, if I can just be assured that God will make me whole in that which is left me. Deliver me then, O Lord, from telling you what I will settle for. "Help me to accept the things I cannot change, courage to change the things I can, wisdom to know the difference." In this sense God comes upon each of us to do His work. I think in a most tremendous way He is speaking to the church in the last half of the Twentieth Century. Here is a part of the Reformation. Here is a part of the new age. Here is a part of the new Israel that was promised so long ago. I think if you and I will claim it, we can be assured the wholeness in His name.

## THE THREE D·S

"Therefore I say unto you, what things soever ye desire, when ye pray, believe that ye receive them, and ye shall have them."
(Mark 11:24)

# 6

## Questions and Answers

**Q.** *You speak of God's will and His allowance of some things to happen. Is there a will of the devil? Is there a power of death working against the power of wholeness?*

**A.** We all know we are going to die physically. I hope I have said nothing that would ever alter that. We do not mean by Spiritual Healing that you are not going to die in the physical sense, but we mean by Spiritual Healing that as long as you live, you are going to live and enjoy it.

Now, is there a will of the devil? Yes, there is a will of the devil at work in the world, and it is a very strong power. I do not have time to go into the theology of demonology, but I do believe in the devil, and the reason is that I fuss with him all the time. If you do not have that trouble, then I need to talk to you. If you

## SPIRITUAL HEALING

have found a way to get around the devil, then I'm perfectly willing to sit at your feet, because I would give anything to get rid of the devil, and so would everyone else. Yes, there is a devil. There isn't any question about that, and he is hard at work, and hard at work in the area of Spiritual Healing also. He will tell you again and again when you come to the kneeling rail, "Now, you foolish person, do you believe that it is possible because the man has said something about the power of God, do you believe that you can come and kneel here and receive anything at all?" If you say, "No, I don't believe I can," then you might as well give up and go, because you have given yourself over to the power of the devil. Every time you go to church on Sunday morning and as you begin to come up the steps, the devil says to you, "Do you think you're going to get anything out of this this morning?" You know that fellow stands up there and doesn't have anything to say to you, because the devil has convinced you that he can't speak to you. If you will always say, "Get thee behind me, Satan," you can trim old Satan down to size. Once you do not attack him, he stays right at hand. Many times I've gone into the Spiritual Healing Service, and as I walked from my office over to the Chapel, the devil has walked right with me and says, "You're too tired tonight. You shouldn't have engaged in this. Nothing is going to happen. The crowds going to be real small. It'll be a discouraging thing. If I were you, I wouldn't get too hepped up about this business. Don't you know people are calling it a strange thing? Don't you know that even the Presbyterians sometimes wonder whether or not you're still sensible?" I have to fight that doggone guy all of the time, constantly, and the only time that I have any fun is when I all of a sudden say, "Get going." Yes, there is a real devil, but I do not believe, however, that there is a power of death working against the power of wholeness. If I understand what you mean by this question when you raise it, the power of death, I believe that all of us die physically, but I don't believe that there is a power of death in the sense that there is a power of wholeness. I do not believe that the devil nor death has equality with God and life, so the thing that is emphasized in the healing ministry is God's over-arching purposes for your life, whether it is here or in the next world.

**Q.** *How can a person thus prepare himself to be open for and receive healing during a healing service?*
**A.** I am glad that question came up. First of all, let me say, "Expect things to happen!" Go with great expectation! Whatever you need, maybe you don't know what you need, but expect something to happen. Should anyone come to a healing or the kneeling rail without being conscious of any need? My answer is yes, indeed, for I do not know anyone whom I have met who does not have a need. You may not have any physical need. You may not have any mental need, but I do not know of anyone who does not have some spiritual need. So everyone may come. You may be very conscious, extremely conscious, of some need physically, or mentally, or spiritually. Emphasize as you come, "Lord, heal me. Make me whole." Don't pray, "Make me well." Pray for wholeness, and expect something to happen. When you get up from kneeling, give thanks to God for what has taken place in your life. Note the changes, as imperceptibly as they may be. Do you have a better mental

peace than you had before you knelt there? Do you feel more calm? Here has begun a healing. Do you feel all of a sudden in your system, tension having been relieved? You are no longer tight or tense? There is a relaxation in the whole physical being, and how about the new attitude with which you walk back the aisle? The interior feeling that you are somehow a new person. If you notice these things, immediately thank God for His healing which has begun in you and then watch it day by day, document it very carefully, as though you were watching your weight on the scales. Write it down. Do you have trouble with your hand? Tomorrow you have less trouble, and the next day less than that. The pain in the elbow is not nearly as bad today as it was yesterday? You no longer bear that resentment against that uncle who gypped you out of part of the inheritance of the family. It doesn't make any difference to you anymore. All of a sudden it has been completely delivered from you. At that point you stand victorious, "erect, facing the heaven of all created forms, God's masterpiece." Give thanks to Him for His wholeness given unto you.

**Q.** *How would you present your ideas to a dedicated M.D. who has no religious creed, but a sincere love of mankind?*
**A.** You're going to be surprised at my answer. I'd take him fishing. That's exactly what I would do. I would say, "Doc, how about going fishing with me, sit out here a long time with the pole, and hope that no bites come." The reason is that what you are doing is developing a companionship, a trustworthy rapport, and ultimately I can talk to that dedicated doctor about spiritual things, but I can't do it until I have him

## Questions and Answers

in my circle. A person who is irreligious, still with a very great dedication to humanity, is a very difficult kind to spiritualize. You must relate somehow to that person through your personality first of all. I would take him golfing or take him out and buy him a filet mignon with onions french-fried and mushrooms all over the top. Then after he exclaimed his delight over the wonderful meal, I would say to him, "Let's do it again, Doc." As we keep this partnership going, ultimately there comes the occasion when all of a sudden he will ask the question. He will say, "How did you ever get interested in that 'kooky' business of spiritual healing? You seem like such a nice fellow. How did you ever in the world get led off on that tangent?" That is exactly the question I want, especially from this man, because he has opened the door and watch me wade through it. This is precisely the way I would handle this dedicated man who is irreligious.

**Q.** *Do you believe any committed Christian has the privilege of laying on hands in a prayer group when a minister is not present?*

**A.** My answer is yes, even if a minister *is* present. Let me take from James 5:13-16 to give you the Biblical answer.

> "Is any among you afflicted? let him pray. Is any merry? let him sing psalms. Is any sick among you? let him call for the elders of the church; and let them pray over him, anointing him with oil in the name of the Lord: And the prayer of faith shall save the sick, and the Lord shall raise him up; and if he have committed sins, they shall be forgiven him. Confess your

## Spiritual Healing

faults one to another, and pray one for another, that ye may be healed. The effectual fervent prayer of a righteous man avileth much."

**Q.** *When is the laying on of hands required beyond intercessory prayer?*
**A.** At any moment in the life of an individual when there seems to be, on the part of that individual, a desperate need and a request for something to take place in his life. We have a young man in our church who was working in an airport. One day he was working alongside a fellow who had a very serious carbuncle on his arm. After showing it to the boss, the boss said, "You quit right now, and, Ash, you take him in to the doctor in North Canton because there are blue streaks running down from that carbuncle, running down his arm." The man relates this story himself. As they started to North Canton, the man was in very severe pain. The young man from our church said to me, "I realized that if I really believed in what we had been talking about in Spiritual Healing, I could do something about it. I pulled the car over and asked him if he believed in prayer." The fellow said, "Yes." Ashley asked, "Do you care if I put my hand on your arm as I pray for your healing?" He put his hand over on his fellow workman's arm and prayed, "Oh Lord, deliver my friend of this pain. Deliver him of the core of this carbuncle." He said to me, "When we opened our eyes, you never saw such a thing in all of your life! That thing had let go, and the blood, the matter, and the core had come out!" They went on to the doctor, of course, who looked at the arm and said, "There isn't anything I can do. It's already been done. I don't know when this happened, but when the core came

out, that was it. You'll be fine. We'll just put a gauze bandage on it." As fantastic as that sounds, it's not my story. It is the story of one of the fellows who himself had been healed.

## ABOUT THE AUTHOR

George E. Parkinson, A.B., S. T. B., Div. M., D.D.
Christ United Presbyterian Church
Tuscarawas Street, Canton, Ohio
Received honorary degrees from
Grove City College
Wooster College
Rio Grande College
Malone College
Author of widely-read papers that include
"Praise and Protest"
"Stop Here for Awhile"
"The Plus and Minus of Life"
"Antidote to Anxiety"
Member of the Board of Trustees
Muskingum College
Malone College

**DATE DUE**

1340

248.2
Par

Parkinson, George E.

Spiritual Healing

DEMCO

*Property of*
**HOLY TRINITY LUTHERAN CHURCH**